MW01138274

ST. AUGUSTINE ACADEMY PRESS

*About **Mother Mary St. Peter:***

Born Jane Lansdowne in England in 1841, from an early age she was educated by the Dominican Sisters in Stone, Staffordshire. She then joined the Society of the Holy Child Jesus, which was still in its infancy, having been founded by Cornelia Connelly in 1846. She was admitted as a postulant in 1862, professed her vows in 1864, and was a well-beloved teacher for many years in the Convent schools. In 1876 she was chosen as Prefect for a new school in Paris, but to her great disappointment, she was unable to take the post, and instead was sent in 1885 to America, where she taught in Nebraska, Minnesota and Wyoming before returning to the motherhouse in Sharon Hill, Pennsylvania in 1897. Here she took up writing as a way of helping to raise money for building the chapel there. "Isn't God good to let me work on these little books?" she once said. "I always wanted to write books on Christian Doctrine and now at the end He is graciously allowing it." She kept up her work until the day she died, writing over a dozen books and plays, the last of which had to be finished by a fellow sister upon her death in 1906.

*About **Mary the Queen:***

Though not Mother Mary St. Peter's first attempt at writing, *Mary the Queen* was the first of a series of 8 books she wrote on Christian Doctrine, which we have named "*The Seat of Wisdom Series*," in honor of Our Lady. This book is a wonderful introduction for young people to the traditions of our Church regarding the life of Mary, from her Immaculate Conception to her Assumption into heaven. It is also an introduction to the various titles by which we call on our heavenly Mother, which will later be expanded in *The Queen's Festivals*.

THE SEAT OF WISDOM SERIES

Mary the Queen

A Life of the Blessed Mother for her Little Ones

by

MOTHER MARY ST. PETER

of the Society of the Holy Child Jesus

edited by

LISA BERGMAN

and

DAVID BRANDT

2016

ST. AUGUSTINE ACADEMY PRESS

HOMER GLEN, ILLINOIS

This book is newly typeset based on
the edition published in 1905 by Burns & Oates.

The text has been modified in places in order to render it more
accessible to modern readers; this was done with great care and
sensitivity toward the age of the material, in order to maintain
respect for the era in which it was written, as well as to
preserve the original writer's voice.
Though the wording has been thus modified, the content itself has
not been changed in any way, except to add Our Lady of Fatima.

All scripture quotations taken from the Douay-Rheims Bible.

Nihil obstat:

REMIGIUS LAFORT, S.T.L.,

Censor

Imprimatur:

✠ JOHN M. FARLEY,

Archbishop of New York

New York, August 15, 1905.

This book was originally published by Benziger Brothers in 1905.
This edited and annotated edition ©2016
by St. Augustine Academy Press.
Editing and Notes by Lisa Bergman and David Brandt.

ISBN: 978-1-936639-61-8
Library of Congress Control Number: 2016940271

Those illustrations found on pp.ii, 13, 29, 34, 40, 45, 51, 56, 62, 69, 87
and 90 are the original illustrations found in the 1905 edition; they have
been retouched with the addition of hand tracings
by artist Erin Bartholomew ©2016.

Contents

Preface

EARS AGO, I came across an old Benziger Brothers book at an estate sale called *The Laws of the King*, written by "a Religious of the Society of the Holy Child Jesus." A brief glance at this little book about the Ten Commandments reminded me quite a bit of my favorite author, so I picked it up, thinking it would make a great addition to our books.

Upon closer inspection, however, I found that, while the subject matter and treatment were excellent, much of the language—as one might expect for the era in which it was written—was archaic in ways that are no longer charming to our modern ears. Many passages required several readings to be fully understood. And though her writing was doctrinally sound, and each commandment was well explained, her particular style of "chattiness" felt awkward and even off-putting at times. No children I knew would enjoy reading this book as-is. And that was that.

Time passed, and I kept pulling this book off my shelf and looking at it wistfully, wishing I could make it work somehow. Then I would read a few passages, cringe, and put it back on the shelf.

But one of those times I had an inspiration: I thought I'd see if I could discover more about this anonymous author. How glad I am for that momentary thought! I discovered not only her true name—Mother Mary St. Peter—but also the fact that she had written an entire series of eight books on similar subjects, all highly valuable for the fact that many are undertreated—or even neglected altogether—by modern catechesis, especially the one you now hold in your hands: the Life of Mary. This little volume holds many important lessons, not only about Our Lady herself, but about the crucial importance of Apostolic Tradition, and how it informs the practice of our Catholic faith in ways we might not expect.

So lest the contents of this series sit collecting dust on my shelf any longer—or worse, that they should not be well-received by our readers—we decided to depart from our standard practice of printing these books exactly as they were written. This does not mean, however, that we have changed any of the content (with the exception of adding a reference to Our Lady of Fatima). In fact, wherever possible, we have kept Mother St. Peter's own words, merely rearranging them more felicitously to make for clearer prose. Yet we have made a point of leaving her *whithers* and *thithers* and such like, because we aren't trying to make her sound like she was writing in this century. We leave it to the parents, if they should wish to modify the language further as they read the following book with their child, to do so "on-the-fly."

The benefit, then, of having carefully ironed out this book, and its companions, is a set of delightful readers for young children that help introduce them to a uniquely wholistic understanding of our Holy Catholic and Apostolic Church—that mystical body which exists not merely in the sum of its members, nor in Divine Revelation alone, nor is it contained solely within the questions and answers of the Catechism; it is made complete by the deposit of faith that has been handed down to us by people as real as you and me.

Yours in Christ,
Lisa Bergman
St. Augustine Academy Press
Feast of St. Mark, 2016

MARY THE QUEEN

Chapter I

Joachim and Anna

any, many hundreds of years ago, there lived in the little town of Nazareth, in the Holy Land, a man named Joachim. He was married to a woman called Anne or Anna, who was as good and holy as was Joachim himself. Nothing was wanting to him of this world's goods, for he owned wide pastures and many flocks in Galilee, besides his house at Nazareth and a dwelling near to the Temple at Jerusalem, whither he could retire with Anna when they went up to keep the great festivals in the Holy City three times a year.

He was descended, too, from the Royal House of David, which was considered by the people to be in itself a great happiness; and his wife, Anna, is said to have belonged to the Tribe of Levi, from whom the priests who served in the Temple were chosen, so that next to the family of David, hers was the noblest in the land.

And yet, with all these good things, Joachim and Anna were not happy. They were not even as happy as people are generally supposed to be, if they serve God with all their hearts, love each other tenderly, and want for nothing. Indeed, the good God had laid a cross upon them which sometimes seemed too heavy for them to bear.

They lived at a time and in a place in which every one was looking forward most anxiously for the coming of the Messias Who had been promised so long ago, when Adam and Eve disobeyed the command of Almighty God by eating the Forbidden Fruit in the Garden of Paradise. Then in order to soften the terrible punishment they had brought upon themselves, our First Parents were told that the seed of the woman should crush the serpent's head.

Later on, a promise was made to Abraham that in his seed should all the nations of the earth be blessed, which showed that the future Saviour was to be of the Hebrew race, since the Hebrews were the descendants of Abraham, and the chosen people of God.

Next, Jacob prophesied that the Messias should come of the Tribe of Juda.

Last of all, Isaias foretold that He should be of the house and family of David, when he said: "And there shall come forth a rod out of the root of Jesse, and a flower shall rise up out of his root;" for Jesse, or Isai, as he is sometimes called, was the father of David.

In consequence of these promises, all the Hebrew or Jewish people—but more especially those of the Tribe of Juda, and most of all the members of the family of David—desired to have children, in the hope that the longed-for Messias might be among them; or at least that some of their descendants might, like holy Simeon, see His day.

But no children came to bless and brighten the home of Anna and Joachim; wherefore their neighbors, perhaps even their kinsfolk, despised them and declared that they were forsaken and forgotten by God. And this shows how wrong it is to judge harshly of others; and how very mistaken such judgments may be. The good God never forsakes those who serve Him faithfully; and instead of forgetting Joachim and Anna, He was all the time teaching them to practice that most blessed virtue of Patience, which was to render them perfect in His sight. For does not the Apostle St. James tell us that "Patience hath a perfect work"?[1]

Now Joachim and Anna needed to become very perfect, and to know how to practise all the virtues in a very high degree. While they were mourning over their childless state, God had determined that these two—whom men believed He had forgotten—should be the parents of *Mary the Queen*.

---

1   James 1:4.

Chapter II

The Coming of the Queen

" 'Mid the carols of shepherds, the bleating of sheep,
   The joy of that birth, Blessed Anne! came to thee,
When the fruits were grown golden, the grapes blushing deep,
   In the fields and the orchards of green Galilee."

o sings Father Faber in his beautiful hymn to St. Anne. But the more generally accepted tradition says that Jerusalem, the city of her Son's love and future sorrow, was the birthplace of the Queen. And here it may be a good idea to explain this word *tradition*, for it is one we often meet, and perhaps do not always understand.

Tradition means, literally, that which is handed down, or over, from one person to another; but by long usage it has come to signify *sayings* that have been handed down from one generation to another, "from father to son," by word of mouth rather than in writing. In the Catholic Church there are many traditions, and I think we may divide them into three classes.

First: many things are taught by the Church which are not *written* in Holy Scripture in so many words, but which we are nevertheless bound to receive as Articles of Faith because they are *defined* or declared by the Church to be such. This is what St. Paul meant when he said, "Stand fast, and hold the traditions."[1]

Next: there are certain pious beliefs held by the greater number of Catholics, and of which the Church, in her practice, seems to approve, but which have never been declared Articles of Faith. The Assumption of Mary the Queen is one of these.[2]

Lastly, there are many stories and legends which have come down to us from very early ages, and upon which our Holy Mother the Church has hitherto pronounced no opinion, leaving us free to accept them or not as we think better.

All that I have told you about St. Joachim and St. Anne belongs to the second kind of tradition; for while the Church has never defined the stories about the birth and childhood of the Queen as Articles of Faith, she has never contradicted them; and they have been received as facts by many wise and holy men.

Now I hope you will understand my meaning when I tell you that according to *tradition* Joachim and Anne

---

1   2 Thessalonians 2:15.

2   At the time this book was written, in 1905, this was true; however, in November 1950, Pope Pius XII defined *ex cathedra* this "pious tradition" as a dogma of the faith in his Apostolic Constitution *Munificentissimus Deus.*

had been married twenty years, and during all that time had never ceased to pray that God would send a little one to lift what they and their people held to be a disgrace from their home.

"The best of good things come to them that can wait," we are told; and so it happened that what was assuredly one of the very best of good things came at last to Joachim and Anne. They were staying at their house in Jerusalem, whither they had come from Nazareth, perhaps to attend at some sacrifice in the Temple; perhaps because Joachim had been warned that a little daughter was to open her eyes to the light in the Holy City. Whatever the reason may have been, there they were; and there, in a little house at the foot of Mount Moriah, at the dawn of morning, was born Mary the Queen.

And to this place, we may be quite certain, came myriads of Angels to gaze in love and admiration on the only stainless blossom that had graced Creation since the Fall, just as, many years later, they will crowd into the Stable at Bethlehem to gaze in awe and adoration on her Son. Many infants had they looked upon in the ages that had passed since Cain and Abel—poor little inheritors of sorrow and death that had come into the World outside the gates of Paradise—and the trail of the serpent was over them all. But no serpent's trail, no spot or stain of sin, had been allowed to come upon Mary. Her lovely soul was all immaculate; she was fair and beautiful as the

Cherubim and Seraphim themselves. And even then the Angels must have called her blessed as they knelt about her cradle and pressed reverent kisses on her tiny hands and feet.

In the Church the birthday of the little Queen will be a joy forever; and therefore, she cries out in her office for the day: "Thy Nativity, O Virgin Mother of God, brought joy into the universal world, since from thee arose the Sun of Justice, Christ our Lord."[1]

There was no Baptism for the little Jewish children, because Our Lord had not yet come to institute the sacraments; but babies were named by their parents with much ceremony and rejoicing when they were eight days old. All the friends of Joachim and Anne who lived in or near Jerusalem must have come to wish joy to her parents, and consider what the infant should be called, for the naming of a child was looked upon as something very important indeed. St. Elizabeth, who was to become the mother of John the Baptist, was Our Lady's cousin, although so much older; and she was most likely there with her husband Zachary, looking with a feeling as much like envy as the saints can know upon the happiness of Anne; for they also were praying that God might send a little one to gladden their home.

When the Jews gave names to their children they were careful to choose one that had some appropriate

---

1   Antiphon for the Feast of the Nativity of the Blessed Virgin Mary, September 8. "*Nativitas tua, Dei Genitrix Virgo, gaudium annuntiavit universo mundo: ex te enim ortus est Sol justitiae, Christus Deus noster.*"

meaning, as was the case with all the names by which
Our Lord was to be known. Thus, *Jesus* signifies
Saviour; *Emmanuel*, God with us; and *Christ* means
anointed. So, when Joachim had to give a name to
Our Lady, he chose, probably by the inspiration of
God, that which beyond all others suits her best, for it
means in Hebrew, Star of the Sea; and in Syriac, Lady,
or Sovereign. Thus, even by name, when only a tiny
baby in her cradle, she was Mary the Queen.

Chapter III

The Presentation of the Queen

URING the lifetime of Moses, "The Great Lawgiver," Almighty God made many laws for His chosen people, which Moses wrote down and gave into the hands of those whom he appointed to teach the Hebrews what they were to do and to believe. One of these laws commanded that the eldest child born into each family should be brought to the Temple, and offered to the Lord. The parents were not obliged to leave the baby, but might give instead a year-old lamb to be offered in sacrifice if they were rich, or two turtle doves if they could not pay the price of a lamb.

There were not temples in every city and village as there are churches nowadays, but only one at Jerusalem, to which all the people were bound to go at least once a year, and whenever they wished to offer sacrifice to God. There were, everywhere, places called *synagogues*, whither they might come to hear the Law and the Prophets read and explained; but for all great ceremonies, such as the presentation of the first born, and the offering of sacrifice, they had to go to Jerusalem.

As Mary was born in the Holy City, her parents remained there until the time came for presenting her in the Temple, which was when she was nearly three months old. They did not leave her then, but made the offering of a lamb, and thanked God with their whole hearts for sending them so great a joy in their old age. Very soon afterward they returned to Nazareth.

You have learned in your catechism that children are bound to go to confession "when they have arrived at the use of reason," and that this is "generally supposed to be at about the age of seven years." Really, people arrive at the use of reason when they are wise enough to know that certain thoughts, words, and actions displease Almighty God—and for that reason, those things must not be thought, said, or done. Some children learn to know right from wrong much earlier than others, and then we say that they are *precocious*, or *sharp*, if we do not wish to use a long word.

Now, not because she was sharp or precocious, but because—since she was all pure and immaculate—Almighty God wished her to know Him, love Him, and serve Him from the very beginning of her life, the little Queen was gifted with reason even before she could speak. And she was gifted with wisdom too, and loved God with her whole heart, and wished to belong entirely to Him.

So when Joachim told St. Anne that it would be well to consecrate her to the Lord in the Temple, that she might grow up in His service, Mary knew and understood quite well what he said; and much as she loved her parents, she was willing and even anxious to go. She was then only a year old, and St. Anne thought her too young to leave her mother's care. So for two more years the little Queen remained at Nazareth, and learned to speak and walk as other children do, and grew every day in age and grace, as we are told later of her Divine Son, until her birthday came.

We know that Anne and Joachim were saints. Great saints they must have been, or Almighty God never would have entrusted to them, as He did, the care of His greatest treasure—the future Mother of His Son. We know, too, that when saints give something they give willingly, and with their whole hearts; but since they are human as well as saintly, they endure the pain of parting with it all the same, if it is something they love very much.

There never had been parents since Adam and Eve who so longed to look upon their first-born as Anne and Joachim had longed to look upon Mary. There never had been, since the first days of creation, a child so lovely or so dearly loved. Nor had any child loved father and mother as the little Queen loved hers. But with every member of this blessed family the holy Will of God came before all things; and it was His Will that Mary should be brought up in His house. So it came

about that Joachim and Anne went down once more to
Jerusalem, and word was sent to the High Priest that
on a certain day a little daughter of the Royal House of
David would be presented for consecration among the
almas or virgins who were educated in the holy place.

We are told that at the time appointed, the priest
stood to receive Mary at the head of the great marble
steps leading to the Women's Gallery in that Temple
which the Jews called "The Glory of the Earth,"
although in truth its real glory had departed long since.
The Ark of the Covenant with the two Tablets of the
Law was lost, and the visible Presence of God could no
longer be worshiped by the High Priest in the Holy of
Holies, "sitting upon the Cherubim."[1]

However, not even Mary might enter the Holy
of Holies, empty as it was. Indeed, she might not go
farther than one of the outer courts of the Temple,
for no women were allowed to set foot within the
holy place.

The old story tells us that Anne had attired the little
Queen in a very beautiful robe, just as we dress our
children in white and crown them with flowers when
Jesus first comes to them in the Sacrament of His love.
It goes on to say that she needed help from no one as
she mounted those fifteen steps, no light labor for a
baby of three; and on reaching the top she gave her
hand to the priest, in token of her willingness to put
herself under his care. He led her to the women who

1 1 Kings 4:4; 1 Paralipomenon 13:6.

lived in one of the buildings belonging to the Temple; and then Joachim and Anne, who had already offered a sacrifice, returned to their home.

We learn from the Gospel that Anna the Prophetess had lived many years in the Temple, and she may have been one of those who welcomed the little Queen, as in later years she was there when the King of kings was carried thither by His Mother for the first time. Holy Simeon, too, is said to have been present; and we may well believe that Zachary and Elizabeth (the future parents of John the Baptist) came from their home in Ain-Karim to meet Joachim and Anne and the gracious little maiden over whose birth they had rejoiced three years before.

So Mary was not left altogether among strangers when she took up her abode in the House of God.

Chapter IV

In the Palace of the King

E must not suppose, because the Queen is said to have been brought up in the Temple, that she lived always in Church.

The Temple at Jerusalem was not in the least like the churches in which we hear Holy Mass and are present at Benediction. It is true that, in a sense, a small portion of it corresponded with our Sanctuary: this was a little building, roofed in with cedar wood covered with plates of gold, and shut off from an outer court called "the Holy" by a most precious veil or curtain, which had been brought from Babylon. (*See diagram, page 25.*)

Into this "Holy of Holies," as it was named, none but the High Priest might enter—and that only once a year. Here the Ark of the Covenant had been kept, with the Rod of Aaron and the two Tablets of Stone, upon which Moses had engraved the Commandments of God. Then, too, there had been a cloud that rested over the Ark on the outstretched wings of two golden Cherubim as a visible sign of the continual Presence of God. But all these things had disappeared long ago, and it would take too long to tell you here how they were lost.

Outside the Holy of Holies was the Sanctuary, or the *Holy*, a court into which the priests entered whose duty it was to offer certain sacrifices; and beyond these were several outer courts, all uncovered, and separated one from the other by porches or colonnades. The outermost court of all was the Court of the Gentiles, beyond whose inner porch no stranger might dare to pass under pain of death. Women were not allowed to enter the actual Temple at all. They had to say their prayers and attend the sacrifices in the Women's Gallery, which was built over one of the colonnades.

But above the porches and beyond the outer wall of the Temple were many buildings which had been erected for various purposes connected with the service of the holy place. The dwellings of the *Almas* or Virgins were in some of these. The little maidens were very carefully brought up by the wives of the priests who lived there, and by women who, like holy Anna, "Departed not from the Temple, by fastings and prayers serving night and day."[1]

So you see, the little Queen was really at school as you are, although the hours and the manner of study were different, and the rules much stricter than yours.

---

1 Luke 2:37.

All the Children of the Temple rose early to sing the praises of God, for the Royal Psalmist had said: "I will prevent the Sun to bless Thee,"[1] and they had to spend the day in learning all those things which the Jewish women were expected to know.   Mary was taught to read and speak Hebrew, because it had been the language of her ancestors, in which the Holy Scriptures—that is, the books of the Old Testament—were written; and Syro-Chaldaic, or Syriac,[2] because this was the language spoken by the Jews in her time. She learned portions of the Holy Scriptures by heart, and to sing Psalms and Canticles—perhaps even to play upon some musical instrument, for the Jews loved the sound of Psaltery and Harp.

Besides all this, she was taught to spin and weave; to fashion garments for herself and others; and to embroider rich hangings wherewith to make beautiful the House of God.

There is a pretty story told how once a curtain had to be woven, and the most skillful among the *Almas* were called upon to do the work. They drew lots for the different colors:—

> "Which should weave the lily white;
> And which should weave the blue;
> Which should weave the gold so bright;
> And which the purple true."

---

1   Wisdom 16:28. The Latin root of the word prevent, *praeveniet,* means literally to "come before"—so that this phrase actually means to rise before the sun.
2   More familiarly known today as Aramaic.

"The purple true" was the color most coveted of all—it was the color worn by kings; and when it fell to Mary's lot, her companions declared that she would one day be a Queen, therein speaking truer than they knew.

Some distaffs used for spinning by the Virgin Mother were kept for hundreds of years in the Church of Jerusalem, and were regarded by the Christians who visited the Holy Places with veneration and love.

Then too the maidens of the Temple had to be practised in the duties of Jewish housewives; for they remained in their early home only for a certain number of years—generally until they were fourteen. They must grind in a hand-mill the corn of which they were to make bread, cook their simple meals, and learn to keep a house in order. And all must be done skillfully and well, since much was expected from those who had been brought up in the House of God.

And of one thing we may be very certain—that whatever the Queen did was done in right royal fashion, and that in every task she fulfilled the mandate of the Holy Ghost: "Whatsoever thy hand is able to do, do it earnestly."[1]

So the years passed on, and Mary continued to grow in age and grace, beloved of God and man, until she was twelve years old. Then, we are told in the old legend, came the first great sorrow of her life: the deaths of Joachim and Anne. They passed away, one soon after

1   Ecclesiastes 9:10.

the other, in the house at Jerusalem where they had remained in order to be near Mary, and Our Lady went to visit them in their last hours. It is said, too, that the Garden of Gethsemane belonged to Joachim, and they were buried there. Their happy souls could not at once enter heaven, since Our Lord had not as yet thrown open the Everlasting Gates; but they descended into the place of rest called Limbo, to await His coming with all the holy persons who were there.

A distaff for use in spinning.

Chapter V

The Espousals of the Queen

EFORE Our Lord came to teach His children the higher ways of perfection, nobody ever thought of devoting their entire lives to the love and service of God as we see so many Religious do now. Children, both boys and girls, were consecrated in the Temple, as you may remember Samuel was in the Tabernacle. The little Joas[1] was saved by being hidden among the children of the Temple when his cruel grandmother, Athalia, sought to take his life; and Our Lady herself, as you have just read, spent the years of her childhood in the holy place. Some especially holy persons like Simeon and Anna also retired to the Temple to spend the last years of their lives in mortification and prayer.

But it was considered to be the duty of everyone, on arriving at a proper age, to marry some other Jew, usually one of the same family and tribe, or at least

1 His story can be found in 4 Kings 11.

nearly related, and themselves to bring up children, from some one of whom it was hoped the Messias might be born.

Now just as the Queen had been preserved from any touch or stain of sin, by what is called the *anticipation of the merits of her Son*, so also was she instructed beforehand in many great and wonderful things which others did not learn until after He Himself had taught them, by word and example, of a more excellent way. So when Mary the Queen reached the age of fourteen, which was the time when Hebrew maidens were expected to marry, she begged that she might remain always in the Temple, and never have to love and serve anyone but her God and Creator. But the priests, in whose care she had been left by her father, did not understand this at all. Perhaps they even took the idea for a mere girlish whim, and thought that it would never do for a daughter of the House of David to behave in a manner such as had never been heard of before.

It is said that many young men of the Tribe of Juda were anxiously awaiting the day when they might apply for the hand of Mary. When it came, the priests who were her guardians were puzzled over how to decide among the suitors who appeared. Some were rich; some held high places; some were comparatively poor and of low estate. But all were of the Tribe of Juda, and some nearly related to the Queen. Among these last was one who was called Joseph. He is supposed to have been a cousin of the Queen, although we are not certain what the degree of kinship really was. Perhaps he was—in this world's goods—the very poorest, and probably of them all he was the oldest, for he is always represented as well on in years.

He presented himself with the others, but the priests saw nothing in him that might seem to mark him out as being worthy to become the spouse of their precious charge. Indeed, they would very likely have preferred to bestow her on one who was wealthier and better known in the world. But the judgments of God are not as the judgments of men, and certainly His views as to the fitness of things do by no means resemble ours. The priests at last found it impossible to decide amongst the suitors, and not wishing to give offense to any, they besought of the Lord that He would settle the question, so that a proper choice might be made. Then they told each of the suitors to bring a staff—the kind used for walking with, in those days of long journeys on foot—and to leave it in the Temple until morning; and this was done. Little they dreamed that one among them was to become the spouse of the Queen of men and angels, and foster-father of the Incarnate Word.

When the priests came to examine the staves in the morning, one—and only one—was found covered with flowers, the lovely pink blossoms of the almond tree. And it was that which bore the name of Joseph, the carpenter from Galilee.

If they were disappointed, as was probably the case, they had to make the best of it, since the Almighty had so clearly manifested His Will.

Though her one wish was that she need not marry at all, Mary knew, just the same, that obedience was the first duty God required at her hands, and she submitted in this, as in all things. After all, she lost nothing, but rather gained a great deal, as they always must who resign themselves entirely to Him. For Joseph prized and honored the holy state of virginity as did the Queen of Virgins herself, and was inspired by God to promise that he would love and care for her as for a most dear sister, who might serve her Lord and Creator in the way that should seem to her best.

Now just as there were no Religious—that is, no monks and nuns making vows and living in community—before Our Lord came, so there were no sacraments by which grace could be conveyed to men's souls. Matrimony, therefore, was not a sacrament, nor was marriage a religious ceremony celebrated as it now is—or ought to be—in church. Weddings were kept with festivities that lasted for more than a week, and the relatives of the bride and bridegroom came with their neighbors and friends to take part in the rejoicings that went on.

As all the ceremonies and festivities were prescribed either by law or the customs of their people, Our Lady and St. Joseph were careful to comply with them. As soon as they were over, Mary said farewell to the

Temple which had been her home for so many happy years, and to the friends whom she had loved so long; and the two holy spouses went to Nazareth, there to take up their abode in the cottage which had belonged to Joachim and Anne.

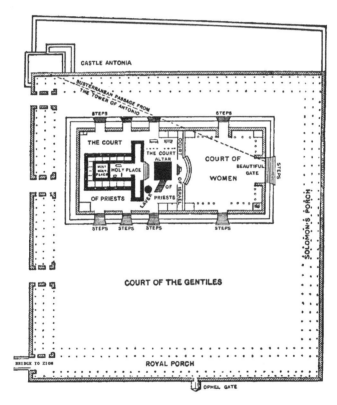

Diagram of the Temple at the Time of Jesus

Chapter VI

The King's Message

HE house to which St. Joseph led Our Lady in Nazareth was not only unlike the magnificent Temple in Jerusalem, but it in no way resembled any dwelling you have ever seen. Indeed you would look upon it as most unworthy to become the palace of the Queen. But it was chosen for her by God, and—once more—His judgments are altogether different from ours. And it must also be said of Our Sovereign Lady, as her Divine Son later said of Himself, that her kingdom was not of this world.

The sun of Palestine is very hot; and people even now build their houses against a rock, or the side of a hill, when they can conveniently do so, for the sake of coolness and shade. If the house can be raised in front of a cave or hollow, so much the better, as this gives an extra room at less trouble and expense. The cottage at Nazareth was arranged in this way.

A little house consisting of two rooms, both small, but one larger than the other, and having a flat roof, stood against the hill on which the City was built. Leading from this, by a step or two, were two more rooms—or rather caverns—connected by a passage, all hollowed out of the hill. These caverns are still shown, and the farthest in is called "Our Lady's Kitchen." Here it was that the Holy Child must often have helped His Blessed Mother in her household tasks when He lived at Nazareth with His parents and "Was subject to them."

In the whole house there was only one window, set high up in the wall. There was no glass in that, for glass was much too expensive a luxury to find in the home of a poor carpenter, had it even been used for windows at all in those days. A wooden trellis that helped to keep out the sun was fitted into the open space in the wall; and when cold winds blew, or the rain beat in, which seldom happened, Our Lady hung up a mat woven of palm leaves, as I believe is done to this day in the East. How the inner rooms were lighted I cannot tell you. As far as we can judge they had neither windows nor doors.

A beautiful church called the Church of the Annunciation stands over these grottoes; but the little cottage built against the mountain side was, very many years later, carried by angels into Italy, and you have often heard of it as the Holy House of Loreto. Some day you will read the story of how it was taken away, but we must not stop for that now.

At the distance of a few paces up the little street stood the workshop of St. Joseph: an open shed, also built against the hillside. Here it was that the descendant of the Kings of Juda plied hammer and saw making stools, and benches, and rude plows for the people of Nazareth—those people who were to look everywhere for the Messias except in their midst, and were to despise Him, because to them He was only "The son of the carpenter," whose father and mother they knew.

And how little they dreamed in Nazareth of the marvelous things that were being done in their midst, when

> The Angel Gabriel was sent from God into a City of Galilee called Nazareth, to a Virgin espoused to a man whose name was Joseph, of the House of David, and the Virgin's name was Mary.
>
> And the Angel being come in, said unto her: Hail, full of grace, the Lord is with thee: blessed art thou among women.[1]

Little they dreamed that He, whom they were to call the son of the carpenter, was in reality the only-begotten Son of God; and that He would not come down to live and suffer and die for us until the little maiden in the carpenter's cottage should have consented to become His mother—so great was His reverence for the Queen.

Mary "having heard was troubled," St. Luke's words tell us; "and thought with herself what manner

---

1 Luke 1:26-28.

of salutation this should be."[1]   It seems strange, at first sight, that Mary should have been troubled by the salutation of the Angel, especially as he came directly from God. Some holy persons have believed that she had often been visited by heavenly messengers in the Temple; and that, as Gabriel was almost certainly her Guardian Angel, she must have known him very well.

But messengers sent from God rarely praise people to their faces, and flatter them—never. Yet what praise could be greater than this: *"Hail, full of grace, the Lord is with thee."* The trouble was not to last long.

> And the Angel said to her, Fear not, Mary, for thou hast found grace with God;[2]

He went on to tell her:

> The Holy Ghost shall come upon thee, and the power of the Most High shall overshadow thee. And therefore also the Holy which shall be born of thee shall be called the Son of God.[3]

The Angel also told Mary that her cousin Elizabeth was to be made happy by the birth of a son in her old age.

> And Mary said: Behold the handmaid of the Lord: be it done to me according to thy word.[4]

...And the Word was made Flesh, and dwelt among us.

---

1   Luke 1:29.   2   *Ibid.*, 30.   3   *Ibid.*, 35.
4   *Ibid.*, 38.

Chapter VII

The Visit of the Queen

And Mary rising up in those days went into the hill country with haste, into a city of Juda. And she entered into the house of Zachary and saluted Elizabeth.[1]

ACHARY and Elizabeth are believed to have lived in a town called Ain-Karim, six miles to the west of Jerusalem. As there were a great many priests, but only one Temple wherein sacrifice might be offered, the priests of a certain rank took it in turn to perform the sacred rites. These turns came in regular order according to the rank, or *Course*, of the priest—that is, the order of his descent from the family of Aaron. Zachary was of the family, or course, of Abia. His turn came about six months before Gabriel had been sent to the Queen, and he had to remain at the Temple for a week. There he would offer the *holocausts*, or burnt offerings, which were a figure of the sacrifice one day to be offered by

1   Luke 1: 39-40.

Our Lord on the Cross. It was also his business to trim the lamps on the seven-branched candlestick, to renew the loaves on the altar of shew-bread (which were a figure of the Most Blessed Sacrament) and to burn incense on the proper altar. These duties were performed in the "Holy," or "Sanctuary," a place which was only slightly less sacred than the Holy of Holies, and could be entered by no one but the priests.

Zachary was offering incense in the "Holy Place" when suddenly the Angel Gabriel appeared to him and told him that his wife Elizabeth should have a son in her old age; that his name should be called John; and that he would "be great before the Lord."[1]

Zachary was "just before God" and "walking in all the commandments of the Lord without blame;"[2] but his faith was not perfect. He said to the Angel: "Whereby shall I know this?"[3] which shows that even very good people may, and do, commit faults sometimes. What follows shows that such faults are punished, and pretty severely too.

The Angel answered that what he had foretold should surely come to pass; but that because he, Zachary, had doubted, he should be struck dumb until the birth of his son. When Zachary came out of the Sanctuary he was unable to speak, and the people said that he must have seen a vision. He returned to Ain-Karim and made known to Elizabeth all that the Angel had said. You may imagine how happy she was.

1 Luke 1:15.   2 *Ibid.*, 6.   3 *Ibid.*, 18.

Six months later Gabriel bore his message to the Queen and told her at the same time that Elizabeth was to have a son. Mary must have known her cousin well in the old days in the Temple; she must have loved her dearly too. Therefore, she arose and went "with haste" into the hill country—the only time we hear of her being hurried in her whole life.

I cannot tell you whether or not St. Joseph went with Our Lady to Ain-Karim. Perhaps he could not leave home and business again so soon. But it is certain that the Blessed Mother did not take the long journey through Galilee, Samaria, and a part of Judea, alone. It may be that she joined a company of travelers going to Jerusalem, for many of such were to be found at every season of the year.

One would like to know if the Angel Gabriel, who, when announcing the glad tidings to his Queen and ours, "knew well that his message was a message of God's light to a dark world,"[1] was allowed to whisper of Our Lady's coming visit to Elizabeth. But all the Gospel tells us is: "She entered into the house of Zachary, and saluted Elizabeth."[2] We know that her salutation was, "Peace be with you," because such was the greeting in use among the Jews.

Then Elizabeth was filled with the Holy Ghost; and she cried out with a loud voice and said: "Blessed

---

1   Homily on the Annunciation by St. Sophronius, as found in the office of Matins for December 9.
2   Luke 1:40.

art thou among women; and blessed is the fruit of thy womb. And whence is this to me that the Mother of my Lord should come to me!"[1]

> And Mary said: My soul doth magnify the Lord; and my spirit hath rejoiced in God my Saviour. Because He that is mighty hath done great things to me, and holy is His Name...[2]

and so on to the end of her beautiful *Magnificat* wherein she declares: "From henceforth all generations shall call me blessed,"[3] as they have done, and will do even to the end of the world.

It was only right and fitting that Zachary and Elizabeth should receive a royal gift when the Queen came to visit them, and so it was decreed that in her honor, and in that of her Divine Son, the little John should come into the world free from the stain of original sin. Could any gift be more magnificent— more worthy of the King and His Mother—than that? Excepting, indeed, Mary's own Immaculate Conception, which was reserved for her alone, because she was to be the Mother of God.

Our Lady remained three months at Ain-Karim, and many pretty legends have come down to us in connection with her stay. But I have space only for one. It tells us that our Queen sometimes went to fetch water from a fountain that flowed in a garden belonging to Zachary. It was not that Elizabeth desired such service

---

1   Luke 1:42-43.   2   *Ibid.*, 46, 47, 49.
3   *Ibid.*, 48.

from the Mother of the Messias; nor was there any real need that Mary should render it, since many servants were to be found in the house of the wealthy priest. But, Queen as she was, Mary hated idleness, and loved to serve others as God's great ones always do.

One day, as she sat beside the fountain, the Blessed Mother noticed a small white flower that grew there, and her heart was so touched by its beauty that she thought to gather and keep it for her own. Then came a second thought—of the God who made it, and clothed it with such wondrous loveliness—and she would not pluck it merely to see it wither and die. So she laid her hand upon its snowy petals, and the story tells us that their tips grew rosy at her touch, blushing with pleasure to be so honored by the Queen. And the flower which until then was scentless has shed a sweet fragrance ever since. English children love to tell this story of their own field daisy, which has a sweet, faint odor of its own, and whose tiny petals are often tinged with red. By others the sweet-scented cyclamen is said to have been the flower Our Lady touched; others again claim her special favor for the red anemone which still abounds in Palestine. Who knows but that at some time or other she graciously laid her hand, or smiled, upon them all?

At the end of three months the little John, a saint already, came into the world. Then Zachary's tongue was loosened, and he was filled with the Holy Ghost, and he prophesied, saying: "Blessed be the Lord God of Israel because He hath visited and wrought the redemption of His people;"[1] and so he sang a song of praise to God in the Psalm we know as the *Benedictus*, which, with Our Lady's *Magnificat*, you must learn some day.

And now Mary bade farewell to her cousin, and we do not find that they ever saw each other on earth again. Painters in old Catholic times loved to think that the two holy families met, and to paint pictures of the little King playing with St. John. But since St. Joseph had to take the Child and His Mother, and fly into Egypt, while Zachary, as far as we know, remained in Judea, it is not likely that such meetings occurred. All the Gospel tells us is that "Mary abode with her about three months; and she returned to her own house."[2]

---

1   Luke 1:68.   2   *Ibid.*, 56.

Chapter VIII

The King's Birthday

LTHOUGH the Jews prided themselves on being the chosen people of God, and boasted that among them alone the hoped-for Messias was to be born, they had long since forfeited by their sins the favor of the Almighty, and had over and over again been brought into subjection by the idolaters whom they despised.

At this very time they were living under the dominion of the Romans, who were, indeed, the masters of the whole civilized world. The Roman Emperor was named Caesar Augustus, and he determined to have a census taken of his subjects all over the world in order that he might learn their number, and the amount of taxes that ought to be paid into his treasury. Moreover, he wished to know to what city each man belonged, and thus every one was ordered to repair by a certain date to the town from which his family originally came.

Our Lady and St. Joseph must have known that something would happen to call them to Bethlehem, because the Prophet Micheas had said: "And thou Bethlehem the Land of Juda art not the least amongst the princes of Juda; for out of thee shall come forth the captain that shall rule my people Israel;"[1] meaning that the Messias was to be born there; but they did not know how this was to be brought about. So when the order of Caesar Augustus came, they did not see in it a hard and unreasonable command to take a difficult journey at the worst season of the year, but only the way in which the Will of God was to be fulfilled, and they set about taking it at once.

Many of Our Lady's friends and relations dwelt in Galilee, and there must have been a large party journeying together to Bethlehem, since all who were of the House of David had to go. Very selfish and inconsiderate they were too, for, on arriving at Bethlehem, they appear to have thought only of themselves, and hurried forward to find such lodgings as they might. So when Mary and Joseph reached the city at nightfall there was, in the whole town, no shelter to be had. Then they took refuge in a poor stable—a shed built against the hillside with a cavern behind it—the home already of an ox and an ass, and there, "Mary brought forth her first-born Son and wrapped Him up in swaddling clothes, and laid Him in a manger; because there was no room for them in the inn."[2]

1 Matthew 2:6.   2 Luke 2:7.

So men treated the Son of the Most High, who came to suffer and die that they might enjoy everlasting life. At His birth He found no shelter but a wretched stable, where He was laid in a manger, upon straw. Later on, when He was spending and wearing Himself out for His ungrateful people, their coldness wrung from Him the complaint that while the foxes had holes and the birds of the air nests, the Son of Man had not whereon to lay His Head. And He found no pillow and no bed whereon to die save a crown of thorns and the hard wood of the Cross. Truly "He came unto His own and His own received Him not."[1]

But God never forgets. "When all things were in quiet silence, and the night was in the midst of her course,"[2] "There were in the same country shepherds watching, and keeping the night watches over their flocks."[3]

They were poor, honest folk, those shepherds of Bethlehem, who never expected anything extraordinary to happen to them, but just did their best to serve God in their own simple way. They hoped, as did all their people, that the Messias might soon appear and put an end to the bondage in which their nation was held. Perhaps they were saying to each other that surely now His time had nearly come, when:

---

1 John 1:11.
2 Wisdom 18:14. "...Thy almighty word leapt down from heaven from thy royal throne, as a fierce conqueror into the midst of the land of destruction."
3 Luke 2: 8.

> Behold an Angel of the Lord stood by them, and the
> brightness of God shone round about them; and they
> feared with a great fear. And the Angel said to them:
> Fear not; for behold I bring you good tidings of great
> joy that shall be to all the people. For this day is born
> to you a Saviour who is Christ the Lord.[1]

Then the Angel told the shepherds where to find the little King and His Mother; and there appeared a whole multitude of the heavenly army singing: "Glory to God in the highest; and on earth peace to men of good will."[2]

There were princes and nobles of the House of David in Bethlehem that night. Six miles off, in Jerusalem, was the great evil King Herod, who lived like a pagan while he called himself a Jew. In and about the Temple dwelt the High Priest and his companions, who prided themselves on holding high places in Israel and on their strict observance of the law. And to none of these, any more than to the selfish kinsfolk at the inn, did God make known the coming of the King. The Angels came only to the humble shepherds watching their flocks under the midnight stars.

"And they came with haste, and they found Mary, and the Infant lying in a manger;"[3] and so the Queen held her Court in a stable, and a manger was the throne of her Son.

---

1 Luke 2: 9-11.   2 *Ibid.*, 14.   3 *Ibid.*, 16.

Chapter IX

The Naming of the King

GREAT festival was held in the house of Elizabeth at the Circumcision of her son; and a crowd of friends and relations came together to rejoice when Zachary gave him his name. But when the little King was born in His City of Bethlehem, none knew of it save a few poor shepherds. No grand gathering was made when He received His Name. But that Name had been brought from heaven by Gabriel to Our Lady; and an Angel had said to St. Joseph: "Thou shalt call His Name Jesus. For he shall save His people from their sins."[1] St. Paul declares that "In this Name, which is above all names, every knee shall bow; of those that are in heaven, on earth, and under the earth."[2] And St. Peter tells us "There is no other name under heaven whereby we may be saved."[3]

Mary the Queen knew all this; and, while with the tenderness of her Mother's heart she must have wept

---

1 Matthew 1:21.   2 Philippians 2:10.   3 Acts 4:12.

sometimes over the cold, the manger, and the pain—
for the ceremony of circumcision was painful, even to
the shedding of blood—she knew also that He suffered
because it was His Will, and she would not have had it
otherwise, even if she might.

And how she loved His Name! How she whispered
it over and over again—hundreds of times—in the
forty days that passed before she carried Him for
presentation in the Temple, as she herself had been
carried by Joachim and Anne. A lamb had been offered
by them for the redemption of their little daughter, for
tradition says that they were rich. But Mary was poor;
a Queen indeed, and the Mother of a King, but of a
King who came to teach His subjects to love poverty,
and whose Mother must love and practise it first of all.
So instead of a lamb, St. Joseph carried two turtle doves
to the Temple wherewith to ransom the Redeemer of
the world.

The Gospel tells us that:

> There was in Jerusalem a man named Simeon,
> and this man was just and devout, waiting for the
> consolation of Israel,[1]

as were all the servants of God who lived at that time!
Of course, by "The Consolation of Israel," they meant
the Messias, who, at last, had really come. Simeon had
prayed long that he might see the King, and

> He had received an answer from the Holy Ghost that
> he should not see death until he had seen the Christ
> of the Lord.[2]

---

1   Luke 2:25.   2   *Ibid*, 2:26.

And now the Christ had come into His Temple and
Simeon was drawn thither by the Spirit of God. There
the old man found the Virgin Mother and the Child
Divine; and: "He also took Him in his arms and blessed
God," and said:

> Now dost thou dismiss Thy servant, O Lord,
> according to Thy word, in peace; because mine eyes
> have seen Thy salvation.[1]

He spoke the Canticle which we call the *Nunc Dimittis*,
and which nobody had ever said or heard before.

While St. Joseph and the Blessed Mother were
wondering at the things he said, he blessed them and
said to the Queen:

> Behold this Child is set for the fall and for the
> resurrection of many in Israel; and for a sign that
> shall be contradicted: and thy own soul a sword shall
> pierce.[2]

From that hour there was a new title for Our Lady.
She knew that the sword which would pierce her soul
must reach it through the Sacred Heart of her Son,
and henceforth she was the Queen of Sorrows. Never
through the three and thirty years of His life that were
to come did she lose the memory of Simeon's prophecy.
Thus came the first of her great sorrows to the Queen.

You remember Anna the Prophetess, who for so
long had made the Temple her dwelling-place? She
too had learned the secret of the Messias's coming;
and had, moreover, leave to tell of it, which Our Lady
herself had never done. But that was from humility, for

1 Luke 2:29.   2 *Ibid.*, 34-35.

we do not find anywhere that she had been forbidden to speak. Anna came in, and seeing the Holy Child, "She confessed to the Lord, and spoke of Him to all that looked for the redemption of Israel."[1]

It was not the Will of His Eternal Father that Our Lord should be left in the Temple. The upbringing of the Only-Begotten Son was to be entrusted to no other hands than those of His Virgin Mother and her Spouse. So she carried Him back to Bethlehem, her heart bleeding, it is true; but still with the hope that until the last great parting she might never be separated from Him again.

---

1   Luke 2:38.

Chapter X

The Coming of the Kings

Arise, be enlightened, O Jerusalem, for thy light is
come, and the glory of the Lord is risen upon thee...
And the Gentiles shall walk in thy light, and kings in
the brightness of thy rising...All they from Saba shall
come, bringing gold and frankincense, and showing
forth praise to the Lord.[1]

o sang the Prophet Isaias nearly eight
hundred years before the coming of the
King. Long before that again David had
said: "The kings of Tarsis and the islands
shall offer presents; the kings of the Arabians and of
Saba shall bring gifts; and all kings of the earth shall
adore Him."[2] But the knowledge of God is from
eternity, and He had spoken by the mouth of yet
another prophet as far back as when the Israelites were
wandering in the desert, before even they had entered
the Promised Land, saying: "A star shall rise out of
Jacob, and a scepter shall spring up out of Israel."[3]

---

1 Isaias 60: 1, 3, 6.   2 Psalm 71:10.   3 Numbers 24:17.

Balaam, the prophet who spoke these words, was not a Hebrew, and he spoke them sorely against his will, for so God had ordained. But their memory had remained among his people, and they had been carried into the wandering tribes who dwelt in the far East. They, as well as the Jews, were looking for the Messias. Partly because of their love for studying the heavens, and partly because of the words of the prophecy, they expected that His coming would be made known to them by a star. And so it was; for God will not disappoint the hope of them that trust in Him.

There is a pretty legend—and I cannot assure you of its truth, much as I should like to believe it—that among a certain people to whom the prophecy was known, three of their Magi, or Wise Men, went up every night into the mountains to watch for the coming of the star. For many generations—for hundreds of years in fact—that untiring watch went on, until at last the patience of the watchers was rewarded and the star appeared. The last three watchers, who are believed also to have been kings, saw a new star in the east, and knew that it was the Star of Jacob, for which they and their fathers had been waiting and looking so long. Then straightway, after telling their people, they mounted their camels, and taking servants and such presents as they thought worthy to be offered to a king, they set out to follow the star.

Now I will give you the story as St. Matthew tells it in his Gospel, for in no other words could it be told as well:

> When Jesus therefore was born in Bethlehem of
> Juda, in the days of King Herod, there came Wise
> Men from the East to Jerusalem, saying: Where is
> He that is born King of the Jews? For we have seen
> His Star in the East, and are come to adore Him.[1]

They had followed the star to Jerusalem, and there it
had disappeared, because now they could inquire of
the priests who knew from the prophecies where the
Messias was to be found.

As He whom they were seeking was "The Ruler
of Israel," the Wise Men naturally supposed that He
would be born in the palace of the king; and thither
they went to ask audience of King Herod, who
governed the country under the Romans at that time.

Now the very last thing he wanted to hear of was
a new ruler of Israel, but even he knew that a Messias
was to come. Herod sent for the priests and asked
them where Jesus was to be born, and when they
told him Bethlehem, he directed the Wise Men to
the City of David, bidding them return and tell him
when they had found the King, "that I also may go
and adore Him."

So the Wise Men left the palace to set out again
upon their quest; and:

> Behold the star which they had seen in the east went
> before them until it came and stood over where the
> Child was...And entering in they found the Child
> with Mary His Mother; and falling down they
> adored Him; and opening their treasures they offered
> him gifts—gold and frankincense and myrrh.[2]

---

1   Matthew 2: 1-2.   2   *Ibid.*, 9, 11.

They brought Him the best of what they had; and although they found Him with a stable for a palace, and a manger for a throne, it was all the same. He had already given His gift to them—the priceless gift of faith—so "falling down they adored Him."

And those offerings meant more than they knew, Wise Men though they were. The gold was a symbol of His Kingly Majesty; the frankincense, which signifies "the prayers of the faithful," was a tribute to His Godhead; the myrrh—fragrant and bitter, and used in the embalming of the dead—typified His sacred Humanity; and at least to the King and His Mother, it foreshadowed Calvary and the Cross.

And now the Wise Men, having seen their King and His Mother, would have returned with their tidings to Herod, but, as ever, God watched over His own. Calvary was to come some day, but its time was not yet. Therefore: "Having received an answer in sleep that they should not return to Herod, they (the Wise Men) went back to their own country by another way."[1]

---

1   Matthew 2:12.

Chapter XI

The Flight of the Queen

And after they had departed, an Angel of the Lord appeared in sleep to Joseph saying: Arise, and take the Child and His Mother and fly into Egypt; and be there until I shall tell thee. For it will come to pass that Herod will seek the Child to destroy Him. Who arose and took the Child and His Mother by night, and retired into Egypt; and was there until the death of Herod.[1]

O St. Matthew in his Gospel tells the story of the second sorrow of the Queen. The little King is scarcely two months old when His Mother must fly with Him like a hunted thing, for already the jealousy of the tyrant is aroused, and Herod is seeking the Child to destroy Him.

St. Joseph appears not to have waited a single hour, for: "He arose and took the Child and His Mother by night," setting out on a much longer and more difficult journey than that which the Holy Family had so lately taken from Nazareth. The distance between Bethlehem

1   Matthew 2: 13-14.

and Egypt is nearly three hundred and fifty miles; and the way lay through a sandy desert, for they dared not follow the beaten and more frequented road.

Egypt had long been a refuge for Jews flying from justice—or persecution—in their own land, and in a Hebrew colony settled at Heliopolis, a Temple had been built to the God of Israel soon after the Babylonian Captivity, in imitation of the true Temple at Jerusalem. Mary and Joseph might find friends in the land of exile—they would certainly meet some with whom they could converse in their own tongue—but it would be a land of exile all the same. St. Joseph was not told how long he was to stay; no time was allowed to make provision for the journey. The prospect that lay before her might well have struck with dismay even the heart of a Queen. But Mary was royal in obedience as in all things, and at the word of St. Joseph, she prepared to set forth at once.

The early Christians loved to think and speak about this long and perilous flight of the Holy Family, and many pretty legends concerning it have come down to us from the far-off days when men and women—yes, and little children no older than you are—fought and suffered for the faith, loving and prizing it more dearly because it was so dearly bought. Here is one of these stories for you.

One day the Holy Family was set upon by robbers, one of whom declared that they should not pass until a heavy ransom had been paid. But another, the Captain of the Band, moved by compassion, tried to prevail upon his comrade to let the travelers continue unmolested upon their way. The evil-minded robber was obstinate, and at last the Captain himself paid the ransom demanded, and, moreover, led the weary wayfarers to the cavern in which he made his home. He bade his wife give them refreshment and shelter for the night, which the poor woman, who had sorrows of her own apart from the evil courses of her husband, willingly did.

When she saw the wonderful beauty of the Babe in Mary's arms she burst into tears, and said that *her* little son was covered with leprosy horrible to see. The Blessed Mother tried to comfort the mother who was so sorely tried, and told her to wash the poor disfigured infant in the water wherein the Holy Child was bathed, and that then he should be cleansed. The woman obeyed, and as the water which had touched the form of the infant God fell upon that of the robber's son, the leprosy disappeared as though it had never been, and he was healed.

The boy grew up to be a robber like his father, and many years later was taken prisoner and condemned to be crucified in Jerusalem in punishment of his crimes. On that same day was crucified the Lord of Glory, who had not forgotten the little leper of the cave. The grace of repentance touched his heart even at the last moment as he hung upon the cross, and before he died he heard from the lips of his Redeemer the blessed words: "This day shalt thou be with Me in Paradise."[1]

---

1   Luke 23:43.

So, protected from the perils that beset their way, but patiently enduring its privations and difficulties, the travelers reached Heliopolis at last. It is said that a great sycamore bowed its branches to the ground in reverence when the Queen sat down beneath its shade; that a fountain of clear, cool water sprang up for her refreshment close by; and that all the idols in one heathen temple fell down and were broken with a great crash when the true Son was borne into the city in His Mother's arms.

St. Joseph found a cottage in Matarieh, a village not far from Heliopolis, and here were passed the next two, or it may be three, years of Mary's life. Here the Holy Child took His first steps on the earth which He had made; here were spoken the first human words uttered by the Word made Flesh; and here St. Joseph waited, and toiled, and prayed, until news arrived that Herod was dead. Then once more:

> An Angel appeared in sleep to Joseph saying: Arise and take the Child and His Mother and go into the Land of Israel, for they are dead that sought the life of the Child.[1]

While Mary and Joseph were flying with the Holy Child into Egypt an awful deed had been done by order of the savage king in Bethlehem.

> Then King Herod, perceiving that he was deluded by the Wise Men, was exceeding angry; and sending, killed all the men-children in Bethlehem and in all the borders thereof from two years old and under.[2]

---

1 Matthew 2:19-20. 2 *Ibid.*,16.

That was a sad day for the mothers of Bethlehem, and they wept and would not be comforted for their murdered babes. But their Angels rejoiced, knowing that those children were the first martyrs who shed their blood for the little King; and that they would be honored in the Church as "The Holy Innocents" to the end of time.

Chapter XII

The Third Sorrow of the Queen

T is supposed that upon his return to Palestine St. Joseph intended to make his home in Jerusalem, but this was not to be. The son of Herod reigned over Judea, and was little better than his father had been. So once more Joseph received a warning in sleep and, tired as they were, the Holy Family went on to Nazareth. Their house must have been falling to ruins by that time, but they had no thought of complaint. God willed that they should live in Nazareth and not in Jerusalem. So although obedience meant dwelling in a broken-down house—until it could be mended—and, for St. Joseph at least, a toilsome journey to the Holy City three times a year, because it was the Will of God they held it to be the better, and indeed the only, thing to do.

Joseph set himself to his old labors in the carpenter's shop. Mary looked after her little household, ground corn in her hand-mill, cooked the simple meals, and took care of her Son, who grew from day to day in grace and beauty, and was never absent from her side. Perhaps it was now that she wove the seamless garment which is said to have grown with His growth, and for which the Roman soldiers were one day to cast lots on Calvary.

The mothers of Nazareth must have looked with envy upon the Blessed Mother of the King, and tradition tells us that when the boys of the City fell out, or were unable to settle their childish disputes among themselves, they would say: "Let us go to the sweet-tempered Jesus," knowing that His Wisdom and Gentleness would make the rough way smooth. So time went on until the Son of God—and of Mary— had reached His twelfth year. He "Grew and waxed strong, full of wisdom, and the grace of God was in Him. And His parents went every year to Jerusalem at the solemn day of the Pasch."[1]

And now that he was twelve years old He, too, must go to Jerusalem for the festival. The Holy Family journeyed to Jerusalem in company with many others of the inhabitants of Nazareth and spent several days in the Holy City. Sacrifices must be offered, services attended in the Temple, and the Paschal Lamb eaten in compliance with the law. Also there was "The Great Sabbath" after the Feast of the Passover to be observed. That must have been a happy visit for Mary when she showed her Son, the true Paschal Lamb, to

1   Luke 2:40-41.

her friends in Jerusalem. But even then—before its time, one might almost say—the Cross was coming to the Queen, and the third sword of sorrow was about to pierce her heart. For "Having fulfilled the days, when they returned, the Child Jesus remained in Jerusalem and His parents knew it not."[1]

It was the custom for the men to travel in one party by the same road, but a little in advance of the women; so when Mary missed her Son at the gate of the City she thought He had gone forward with Joseph, while St. Joseph believed that He was with her.

> And thinking that He was in the company, they came a day's journey and sought Him among their kinsfolk and acquaintance. And not finding Him they returned into Jerusalem seeking Him,[2]

their hearts torn with anxiety and grief. For three days the search continued, up and down the streets of Jerusalem and in all the houses of their friends, until at last:

> They found Him in the Temple, sitting in the midst of the Doctors, hearing them and asking them questions.[3]

The learned men among the Jews, proud as they were, did not hold themselves above teaching little children. St. Paul afterwards told the Hebrew people that he had been "Brought up at the feet of Gamaliel in this City"[4] (meaning Jerusalem), and Gamaliel we know to have been one of the most learned Doctors, or Teachers, of his day.

1   Luke 2:43.   2   *Ibid.*, 44-45.   3   *Ibid.*, 46.
4   Acts 22:3.

> And His Mother said to Him: Son, why hast Thou
> done so to us? Behold, Thy father and I have sought
> Thee sorrowing.[1]

Who, save His Mother, could have dared to speak thus to the King? But although she did so speak, it was not that she mistrusted Him. All the sorrows she had ever known were as nothing to the agony of that terrible loss; yet through it all she had trusted Him entirely—for was He not her God? But never before had He acted without consulting her—He would not even come to earth from heaven until she had given her consent. Had she in any way offended Him, or wounded His Heart?

Oh, why had He done so to them!

> And He said to them: How is it that you sought Me?
> Did you not know that I must be about My Father's
> business?[2]

And the Gospel tells us that "They understood not the word that He spoke to them."[3]

But one thing they understood—that in the word was all wisdom because He had spoken it.

> And He went down with them and came to Nazareth,
> and was subject to them. And His Mother kept all
> these words in her heart.[4]

---

1 Luke 2:48.   2 *Ibid.*, 49.   3 *Ibid.*, 50.
4 *Ibid.*, 51.

Chapter XIII

The Death of St. Joseph

AND now for eighteen long, happy years peace settled down upon the holy house at Nazareth. Beyond the words: "And He was subject to them," the Gospel tells us nothing of those years. The Holy Child must have helped His Mother in her household labors and, when old enough, helped St. Joseph in his daily toil. He must many a time have fetched water from the fountain, and run on errands through the streets of Nazareth. Perhaps in time the people there might have possessed tools, or boxes, or simple furniture fashioned by the Hands of the God made man! And at least once a year the whole family would have gone up to Jerusalem, where at sight of the Temple the terrible third sword would each time pierce anew the heart of the Queen.

Did she dread, while in the City, to let her treasure out of her sight for a moment, lest she might lose Him once more? Or did He, to console His Mother, assure her that until the time when He must set aside all else to go about His Father's business He would never leave her again? We cannot tell. All we know for certain is that "He went down to Nazareth and was subject to them," and that "He advanced in wisdom, and age, and grace before God and men."

Although the Gospels are silent on the subject, there is one event that we are quite certain must have happened before Our Lord began His public life, and that is the death of St. Joseph. We do not know with equal certainty where or when he died, but it is believed to have been at Nazareth, and when her Divine Son was old enough to take care of the Queen.

And what a death that must have been, in the arms of Jesus and Mary, with companies of Angels waiting to bear the blessed soul to Limbo, the abode of rest. There St. Joseph would meet the Patriarchs and Prophets, and make them happy with stories of the Messias, whom they too might now hope soon to behold. Adam and Eve would learn how the seed of the woman had already begun to crush the serpent's head. David and Isaias and Daniel would hear of the fulfillment of many of their prophecies, and know that many more must shortly be fulfilled. All would rejoice with unspeakable delight in the knowledge that, in a few short years, the Everlasting Portals would be lifted up, and that they would finally enter into the joy of their Lord.

Because of the wonderful peace of his own deathbed, St. Joseph is invoked as the special Patron of a happy death. Let us hope and pray that when the hour of our last passage approaches, he may be near to strengthen and console us; and that Jesus and Mary may be present at our deathbed, as they were present at his.

Chapter XIV

The Queen at the Marriage Feast

HE peaceful, happy life of those years at Nazareth ended at last, and the day came when her Divine Son bade farewell to the Queen. Not that she was never to see or live with Him again, but the time had arrived when He was to go forth among the people, and endeavor by His preaching and miracles to lead them to God. Mary knew that this was the beginning of the end. That when He left her quiet home He was really setting out on the road to Calvary; that upon earth He never could be only and entirely hers again. He asked her blessing and permission to go; then He went to the River Jordan to be baptized by John; into the desert to fast for forty days and nights; and then was tempted by the devil.

How her Mother's heart must have ached to be with Him, to serve Him, even to look upon Him from a distance so that He might not be utterly alone. But this was not to be. Happy Angels came and ministered to Him when His fast was ended, but His Mother must find such comfort as she might in the knowledge that she did His Will.

The Queen did not shut herself up in selfish solitude to mourn over her loneliness, for very soon we read that "There was a marriage at Cana in Galilee, and the Mother of Jesus was there."¹ She would help to make others happy though her heart might be breaking; and she had grown so like her Son during the long years at Nazareth, that henceforth her one desire must be— as His was—to go about doing good. "And Jesus also was invited with His disciples to the marriage,"² for the King had disciples now. Peter and Andrew and Philip and James had been called to follow Him, and His Mother must meet Him in a crowd.

I cannot tell you who were the bride and bridegroom whom the Creator of the universe and the Queen of Angels honored with their company. They lived in Cana of Galilee, about six miles from Nazareth, and they cannot have been rich, for the wine they had provided was not sufficient for their guests. "And the wine failing, the Mother of Jesus said to Him: They have no wine."³ She could not bear to see her friends put to shame upon their wedding-day. "And Jesus said to her: Woman, what is it to Me and to thee? My hour is not yet come."⁴

1 John 2:1. 2 *Ibid.*, 2. 3 *Ibid.*, 3.
4 *Ibid.*, 4.

You must not suppose that Our Lord showed any want of reverence to His Blessed Mother in addressing her as "Woman," although it sounds harsh to us. The word which we translate by the English "Woman" was used in Hebrew in speaking even to queens. And our Queen understood. She said to the servants, "Whatsoever He shall say to you, do ye,"[1] never for one instant doubting that He would do her will.

Then He told them to fill the water-pots that stood there with water, and they filled them up to the brim. And He told them to "Draw out now and carry to the chief steward of the feast."[2]

And behold! when the chief steward had tasted it, he found that the water had been changed into wine, and that of a much better quality than had been provided at first, wine worthy to be the wedding present from a King to His friends. "This beginning of miracles did Jesus at Cana of Galilee,"[3] at the bidding of His Mother.

1 John 2:5.   2 *Ibid.*, 8.   3 *Ibid.*, 11.

Chapter XV

The Queen at Capharnaum

OU have often heard of the Sea of Galilee, sometimes known also as the Lake of Genesareth, whereon Our Lord worked many of His miracles, and on which His Apostles plied their trade of fishermen before He called them to follow Him. On the northern shore of this Sea of Galilee stood the City of Capharnaum, and here lived Peter and Andrew, Matthew, and James and John. After the marriage at Cana, Our Lord went with His Blessed Mother and His disciples to this city, and thence to Jerusalem, because: "The festival of the Pasch was at hand."[1]

I cannot say for certain that the Queen went to Jerusalem then, as women were not bound by the law to go, although the devout among them frequently went. But after the Pasch she went back to her house at Nazareth. And after remaining for a season in Judea,

---

1   John 2:13.

working many miracles there, Jesus came thither also. While at Nazareth, Our Lord went into the Synagogue one Sabbath day to explain the Scriptures to the people, as it was the custom for men who had reached the age of thirty to do. His fellow-townsmen, when they heard Him speak, were astonished at His wisdom, but they were jealous and angry too. They said: "Is not this the son of the carpenter, whose father and mother we know?"[1] and were furious at His trying to explain the Law and the Prophets to them. Our Lord told them that a prophet is not without honor save in his own country and among his own people; and then they dragged Him to the brow of a hill and would have cast Him down headlong, but He passed through their midst and went away.

From that time Our Lord never again made His home in Nazareth. Once more He had "come unto His own, and His own received Him not."[2] Nay, more: they cast Him out from among them; and so the ungrateful people lost both the Messias and the Queen. Henceforward when He returned in the course of wanderings into Galilee it was at Capharnaum, not at Nazareth, that He stayed, and the City by the sea soon became known among His disciples as "His own town."

The Gospels tell us little about what happened to the Queen during the public life of her Son. We know that a company of devout women gathered about her, and that with them, she often went with Our Lord

---

1 John 6:42.   2 *Ibid.*, 1:11.

on His many missions of mercy, rendering to Him such loving service as she might. Once, when Jesus was preaching to a multitude, someone told Him that His Mother and brethren were without seeking Him. Then He pointed to His disciples, saying: "Behold My Mother and My brethren. For whosoever shall do the will of My Father who is in heaven, he is My brother, and My sister, and My mother,"[1] thereby declaring her right to her glorious title, for who ever did the Will of the Father in heaven as perfectly as did Mary the Queen?

And here I should explain that the word *brethren* as used in the Gospel is not intended to express literally children of the same father and mother. We know that Our Lord had no brethren in that sense. It is used to signify any near relatives just as the French use the word *parent* even now.

In church no doubt you have often heard a preacher address a whole congregation as "Dear Brethren," but nobody supposes that he is speaking to the members of his own family only.

On another occasion a woman in the crowd about Jesus, astonished at His wisdom and holiness, cried aloud that His Mother must be blessed indeed. And He answered: "Yea, rather blessed are they who hear the Word of God and keep it,"[2] thereby pointing out that Mary's sanctity was far more blessed than even the glorious privilege of being the Mother of God.

1   Matthew 12:49-50. 2   Luke 11:28.

And that is all. From Passover to Passover the years sped on and, daily and hourly, the shadow of the Cross grew darker, and sharper and sharper became the sword of sorrow that was fastened in the heart of Mary the Queen.

Chapter XVI

The Way of the Cross

UST twenty-one years had passed away since Mary and Joseph had first taken the little King to Jerusalem at the solemn festival of the Pasch, and after they had "fulfilled the days, when they returned, the Child Jesus remained in Jerusalem, and His parents knew it not."[1] Many sorrows had the Queen known since then, but never one so terrible as that of the three days' loss. Now she came again to Jerusalem to keep another Passover, and to endure suffering such as had not entered into the heart of man to conceive.

I cannot tell you where the Mother of Sorrows dwelt during that first awful Holy Week. It may be that she abode in the house of Joachim and Anna at the foot of Mount Moriah; or perhaps, as some suppose, she accepted with Jesus the hospitality of Lazarus and his sisters Martha and Mary at Bethany. One thing only

---

1   Luke 2:43.

is quite certain, and that is that Mary was at Jerusalem when her Son suffered and died. It is believed that she, with the holy women, was in the same house on Holy Thursday when Our Lord ate the Last Supper with His disciples and celebrated the first Mass, but in a separate room. She must have followed Him in spirit to the Garden of Gethsemane, and shared in that Agony in the grotto which she might not witness with her bodily eyes.

And like Him she was alone. St. Joseph was gone to his quiet rest; and if, after His betrayal by Judas, "The disciples, leaving Him, all fled away,"[1] it is not likely that they took thought for His Mother, when in their selfish terror they forsook her Son. It was known in the city that He had been taken by the soldiers at midnight, and was to be tried before Annas and Caiaphas in the morning. And though she was likely unable to obtain admittance into the Court of the High Priest, she must have been very near.

How her soul was wrung when she heard of the denial of St. Peter. Every blow inflicted on her Divine Son must have fallen on her bleeding heart. When "The whole multitude of them, coming up, led Him to Pilate,"[2] she was there. She saw Him sent back by Herod through the streets of Jerusalem clothed in a white garment in derision, as one who had sought to make himself king. She heard the words addressed by Pilate to the people: "You have a custom that I should

1   Mark 14:50.   2   Luke 23:1.

release one unto you at the Pasch; will you therefore that I should release unto you the King of the Jews?"[1] And she heard the mad cry of the people—those same people whom He would have gathered as the hen gathers her chickens under her wings, and they would not—"Not this man, but Barabbas."[2]

And Barabbas was a robber.

> Then therefore, Pilate took Jesus, and scourged Him. And the soldiers platting a crown of thorns, put it upon His Head; and they put on Him a purple garment.[3]

Then the governor, since he "found no cause in Him," brought Jesus, clothed as a mock king and crowned with thorns, once more before the people, and said: "Behold the Man!" And they all, urged on by the Chief Priests and the Pharisees, answered, saying: "Crucify Him! Crucify Him!"

> Then therefore he delivered Him to them to be crucified; and they took Him and led Him forth.[4]

Then began that Way of the Cross which, for love of Jesus and Mary, we follow as well as we may when we make the Stations. You know, for unless you are very young indeed, you have learned by heart, how "Jesus was condemned;" "Jesus was loaded with His Cross;" "Jesus fell for the first time under the Cross;" and then—the Fourth Station which moves our hearts more even than the others—"Jesus meets His Blessed Mother."

---

1   John 18:39.   2   *Ibid.*, 40.   3   *Ibid.*, 19:1-2.
4   *Ibid.*, 19:16.

What a meeting that was! Many a time before had
Mary met Jesus in Jerusalem. When she found Him in
the Temple after the three days' loss; later, when as boy,
and youth, and man, He had come up with her to the
solemn festivals; and later still, during the three years
of His public life, when the multitude—those who now
followed Him with scoffs and jeers, and cries of *Crucify
Him! Crucify Him!*—waylaid Him with their sick, and
blind, and lame, that He might heal them, because they
knew that "He went about doing good."[1]

Well may the Church apply to Mary the words
of Holy Writ: "O all ye that pass by the way attend;
and see if there be any sorrow like unto my sorrow."[2]
Sorrow like unto hers in truth there could be none,
but the brutal soldiers and the cruel crowd felt no
pity for the Queen. With savage blows they forced
her Son to continue His way, and "There followed a
great multitude of people and of women who bewailed
and lamented Him."[3] With them, too, followed His
Mother, who neither lamented nor bewailed.

"And when they were come to the place which is
called Calvary, they crucified Him there."[4] She saw
the soldiers tear the rough woolen garments from His
stiffening wounds. She saw Him thrown down and
stretched upon the Cross. She heard the blows of the
hammers, as great iron nails were driven into His Hands
and Feet. How did she bear it? Can even the Angels of

---

1   Acts 10:38.   2   Lamentations 1:12.   3   Luke 23:27.
4   Luke 23:33.

God understand? We know *why* she bore it, and would not have had it otherwise if she might—because He willed it so. O Children, when shall we ever learn the blessedness of entire and absolute conformity to the Holy Will of God!

At last the Cross was lifted, and fell with a horrible jolt into the hole prepared for it, and then the three hours' agony began—for the Mother as well as for the Son. He spoke to her once, when He gave her to the care of the Beloved Disciple; and did not this very fact remind her that He was leaving her forever? No; not entirely. She knew that to the end of time He would remain with us in the Sacrament of His Love. She knew that in a few short years He would call her to reign with Him in Heaven. But the comfort of such knowledge could hardly come to her then.

The Seven Last Words had been spoken; the earth shook, the heavens were darkened, and bowing His Head with a great cry Jesus gave up the ghost. The people, terrified by the earthquake and the darkness, "went home striking their breasts."[1]

The Chief Priests, too, must have been frightened enough, but Satan had entered into their hearts; they did not do penance.

The Great Sabbath was at hand, and they hurried back to the city to prepare for it. Joseph of Arimathea went to Pilate to beg leave to bury the Body of Jesus. Our Lord was taken down from the Cross, and laid in

---

1 Luke 23:48.

the arms of His Blessed Mother. Mary Magdalen and the other holy women brought spices and fine linen wherewith the precious Body was embalmed. It was laid by the Apostles and Joseph of Arimathea "in a new sepulcher, wherein no man had as yet been laid."[1] Then Mary the Queen, with Mary Magdalen and the Beloved Disciple, returned, sorrowful and lonely, to her home.

---

1   John 19:41.

Chapter XVII

The Resurrection

And on the first day of the week, very early in the morning, they came to the sepulcher, bringing spices which they had prepared. And they found the stone rolled back from the sepulcher. And going in they found not the Body of the Lord Jesus. And it came to pass, as they were astonished in their minds at this, behold, two men stood by them in shining apparel, and they said unto them: Why seek you the living among the dead? He is risen—He is not here.[1]

These are the words in which St. Luke tells us how the holy women learned of the Resurrection of Our Lord. Later we find that He, Himself, appeared on the same day to Mary Magdalen, to Peter, and to the Apostles who were gathered—all save St. Thomas—in the upper chamber for fear of the Jews. In neither of the four Gospels do we find one word to tell us that her Risen Son showed Himself to the Queen. Could it be possible that now, when His life of toil and poverty at Nazareth,

1 Luke 24:1-6.

the labors and journeys of His public life, and the bitter sufferings of His Passion were over—now when, if we may dare to say so, He needed her loving sympathy no more—He had forgotten His Mother?

Ah no, Children; never let such a thought enter your minds. Be sure that the first visit of all was paid to her—and the writers of the Holy Gospels felt that there could be no need to tell us so.

What passed on that Easter morning between the Risen King and His Mother in all probability none of them knew—not even John the Beloved; and we do not seek to know. We would not "Pry into the hidden things of God."[1] But if her desolation had been "great as the sea"[2] during the week of His Passion, so also a sea of perfect happiness must have swept over her spirit now. And think how many glad visits must have been paid her as first one and then another—Mary Magdalen, the holy women, Peter, John, and then the Apostles all together—came to tell her, as they surely did, that the Lord had risen. Perhaps even Gabriel was allowed to show himself, as long ago on the first glad feast of the Annunciation, and say once more: *Hail Mary, full of grace, the Lord is with thee.* Truly a grand court was held that day by Mary the Queen.

Then began the forty days before the Ascension—the forty days of His last stay upon earth. Our Lady went with the Apostles into Galilee, where Peter took the miraculous draught of fishes at the command of

---

1　*cf.* Deuteronomy 29:29.　　2　Lamentations 2:13.

his Lord, and was appointed to be the head of His Church.

Last of all she went with her Son and His Disciples to Mt. Olivet upon Ascension Day when "He was raised up and a cloud received Him out of their sight."[1] And then she knew that her Son Jesus—the Babe of Bethlehem, the Boy of Nazareth, the Man-God, who at her word had worked His first miracle at Cana of Galilee—was gone from earth forever. Would He not have remained had she asked Him to stay with her? Father Faber says:

> Why do not thy sweet hands detain
>   His Feet upon their way?
> Oh, why will not a Mother speak,
>   And bid her Son to stay!

And then he tells us why in the next verse:

> Ah, no! thy love was rightful love,
>   From all selfseeking free;
> The change that was such joy to Him
>   Could bring no grief to thee.

He could never know suffering or sorrow, or pain or labor, again. That was enough for her. In silent prayer she went back to Jerusalem with St. Peter and the other Apostles, there to await in the upper chamber the coming of the Holy Ghost, as St. Luke tells us in the Acts of the Apostles:

> All these were persevering with one mind in prayer, with the women, and with Mary the Mother of Jesus, and with His brethren.[2]

---

1   Acts 1:9.   2   *Ibid.*, 14.

Chapter XVIII

The Death of the Queen

N the Day of Pentecost the Apostles and Disciples of Jesus received the Holy Ghost, making those who, during His Passion, were afraid of being known to belong to Him; who retired into the upper room and remained there even after His Resurrection "For fear of the Jews,"[1] into "strong and perfect Christians, and soldiers of Jesus Christ,"[2] so that they were no longer afraid of anybody, but were ready to appear before kings and governors for His Name's sake. They had received, too, the gift of tongues, which means that when they spoke or preached, all the people understood what was said, no matter to what nation those people belonged.

On this first Whitsunday, St. Peter preached to a great crowd composed of "men of every nation under heaven,"[3] who were gathered at Jerusalem for the

---

1 John 20:19.   2 Baltimore Catechism #3, Lesson 15, #670.
3 Acts 2:5.

festival time, and three thousand were converted by his words. Mary the Queen was present at that sermon, and it is said that, later on, when St. Stephen was led forth to martyrdom, she, too, went outside the city with the multitude of the people; and tradition points to a place near the Brook Kedron where she knelt and prayed whilst he was stoned.

She lived in Jerusalem for some time after that—it is not known exactly how long—and then went with St. John to Ephesus, because he had been appointed bishop of that town. We know little of what happened during her stay there; but she must have suffered much at witnessing the idolatry that prevailed.

There was in Ephesus a temple to the goddess Diana, which was very beautiful, and it was famous all over the world. Many persons came from distant parts of Europe to visit this temple and invoke the goddess, and it was the fashion to buy little silver models of the building, or little statues of the goddess herself, and carry them away as keepsakes and presents for friends. There was much to grieve the heart of Mary in the pagan city, although many converts were made there, and the sanctity of their lives was known and honored in the early Church.

Many, many years after the Assumption of the Queen, a wretched man named Nestorius arose who insulted her, and strove to persuade the followers of her Divine Son that she was not truly the Mother of God. The Council in which this evil doctrine was condemned was held at Ephesus, and there a prayer was composed in honor of Our Lady that you know and say every day, and many times a day: the second part of the *Hail Mary*. This was in order that her children might learn to express their faith and atone in some degree for the dishonor done by Nestorius to the Queen.

The Ephesians were furious with the man who had dared to deny that Mary is the Mother of God, and would, perhaps, have torn him to pieces in their anger had not the bishops who were assembled for the Council interfered. However, he died a miserable death later on.

But all this took place some hundreds of years after Our Lady and St. John left Ephesus. This happened when the Blessed Mother felt that her life on earth was drawing to a close, and that very soon she would hear the Voice of Jesus calling her home. Then she wished once more to see Jerusalem, the city of His love and sufferings, and journeyed back to Judea with St. John. There she visited again the holy places—the Temple where He had preached, the supper room wherein the Most Holy Sacrament had been instituted, and the house of Lazarus at Bethany where He had so often lodged. She made the Way of the Cross, walking in the very footsteps of her Son; she stood again upon Calvary, and knelt at the sepulcher wherein His Body had been laid.

And at last the call came. Perhaps the Angel Gabriel brought the message; perhaps Our Lord Himself came

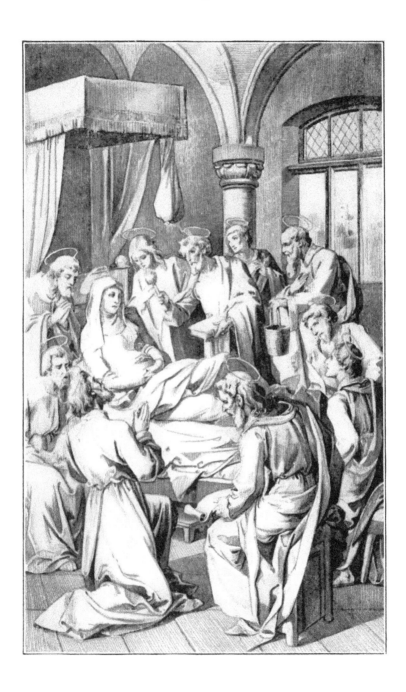

with tidings of release. However, it may have been simply that death was near and she knew it, and longed once more to see and give a farewell blessing to the beloved Apostles of her Son.

They were all scattered—preaching the Gospel and doing their Lord's work in many lands. They learned by inspiration that the Queen was going home and were brought to Jerusalem by the power of God. Just as Philip the Deacon "was taken away by the Spirit of the Lord"[1] after baptizing the treasurer of Queen Candace, and "was found at Azotus,"[2] so, Tradition tells us, the Apostles were found gathered about the deathbed of the Queen.

It seems sad to us that of all the twelve—or eleven rather, for Thomas came late—not one has left for us the story of her passing away. We only know that she died as she had lived, because God willed it—and that she must have been very, very happy to go.

The Apostles and Disciples buried her blessed body in a sepulcher which is still shown as "The Tomb of the Virgin," quite close to the Garden of Gethsemane— but her body is no longer there. Our Lord would not "suffer His holy one to see corruption,"[3] and so after the Apostles had laid their mother in the grave, the Angels came and rolled away the stone from the mouth of the sepulcher, the soul of Mary was reunited to her body, and both were gloriously assumed into Heaven by the power of her Son.

1 Acts 8:39.   2 *Ibid.*, 40.   3 Psalm 15:10.

I told you that St. Thomas arrived too late to see Our Lady die. It is a sad thing to be dilatory—and even sanctity does not immediately cure all imperfections, it seems. In this instance poor Thomas certainly paid the penalty of his fault, if fault it were. Before he reached Jerusalem the Queen had been buried and, strong man as he was, he wept bitterly at the thought that on earth he might never look upon her face again. Peter and John were filled with compassion when they saw his grief, and bade Thomas come with them to the sepulcher. They would roll away the stone, and he should have at least the comfort of kissing her feet, and of gazing upon her beautiful features, although her eyes were closed and her sweet voice silent forever.

But when they came to the place where they had laid her, the stone was rolled away, the linen cloths in which her body had been wrapped alone were lying in the sepulcher, and the tomb was heaped with lilies and roses such as they had never seen before. All the air was filled with exquisite perfume, and heavenly music floated around while an Angel told her children that Mary had been assumed into Heaven by the power of her Son; and that there on a throne of Glory she would reign for all eternity, the Sovereign Lady of Angels and of Men—MARY THE QUEEN.

THE HONORS OF THE QUEEN

Chapter I

The Queen's Festivals

ND now we have finished the story of the life of Mary the Queen. There is very, very much more that you will, I hope, come to know as you grow older and learn to say your prayers—above all the Rosary—with attention and love. I suppose we learn more about our Blessed Mother by saying her Rosary well, than in almost any other way.

Then you will read, and if you read, you must love the Offices of the Church, and what the Holy Ghost teaches about the Mother of the Eternal Son. They are rather difficult for you to understand just now; some of the words you might even find hard to read, so you will have to wait awhile before you can hope to learn much from the Offices of the Church.

The Rosary you can and of course do say; although perhaps not as perfectly as some day you will.

But there are some other ways by which you may gain more knowledge of the Queen—ways that are easy enough even for your little feet to tread, and very pleasant ways besides. One of these is the finding out all you can about her feasts—that is, the days and seasons set apart by the Church as especially belonging to her.

You keep your birthday, do you not, and those of your friends? And you hear grown-up people speak of celebrating wedding-days, and Silver Jubilees, and even Golden Jubilees sometimes. You certainly know something about Thanksgiving Day, Washington's Birthday, and the Fourth of July. All these are festivals; and just as people keep them in honor of their friends, their ancestors, or their country, so do Mother Church and her children keep festivals in honor of Our Lord, His Blessed Mother, and the saints.

When you keep your birthday you like to have a holiday from lessons; you ask your friends to your birthday party; and you look for a birthday present from at least Papa and Mamma, or those who love you best. The making of as much noise as possible seems to be the favorite method of celebrating the Fourth of July; and on Thanksgiving Day people go to church— perhaps—and eat turkey and mince pies.

But how does the Church celebrate her feasts? In this way: If the festival is very important, she bids her children take a rest from all unnecessary servile work, and commands them to hear Holy Mass. These festivals are called Holy Days of Obligation. Six such are observed in America during the year. They are:

- The Immaculate Conception of the Queen, on December 8;
- Christmas Day, or the Nativity of Our Lord, December 25;
- The Circumcision of Our Lord, or New Year's Day;
- Ascension Day, forty days after Easter;
- The Assumption of the Queen, August 15, and
- The Feast of All Saints, kept on November 1.

The feasts of Easter and Pentecost always fall on Sunday, so these days are not called Holy Days of Obligation.

You will easily see, if you think a little, that all the feasts I have mentioned are in some way or other connected with Our Blessed Lady, but two of them—the feast of the Immaculate Conception and that of the Assumption—are entirely her own. Many feasts besides these two are kept in honor of Mary, but only these are Holy Days of Obligation. On the others we are not *obliged* to hear Holy Mass under pain of Mortal Sin; and we may do as much work as our duty may demand. Lessons may be learned, stockings darned, household tasks gone through with as usual—only rather more perfectly, of course. All things must be done "better than well," if possible, on the Queen's Days. And the Church on these days says a special Mass in honor of the Blessed Mother.

Now do not read carelessly, Children, and run off with the idea that Holy Mass is said *to* Our Lady on her feasts. The Mass is a sacrifice, and *sacrifice may be offered only to God.* But in a Mass of Our Lady, particular prayers are said by the priest imploring her intercession; and the Psalms used at the Introit, Gradual, and Tract refer more especially to her.

Devout children of Mary try to hear Holy Mass on all her feasts, and to do something more than usual to please their Mother in Heaven. They bring flowers to her altar; say the Rosary or the Little Office of the Blessed Virgin Mary, or give some alms to the poor. Just think what a delight it would have been to pay a visit or make a present to Mary and the Holy Child at Nazareth! We can do both now by visiting the Blessed Sacrament and the altar of Our Lady, and by making an offering there, or to the little ones of Christ.

At the end of this book you will find a list of the feasts celebrated by the Church in honor of the Queen, and the names of the greater number will show you for what reason each of them is kept. Thus on the feast of the Immaculate Conception we congratulate the Queen on her great privilege of perfect spotlessness and freedom from every stain of sin. Perhaps you might sing:

> "O Mother! I could weep for mirth,
>   Joy fills my heart so fast;
> My soul to-day is heaven on earth,
>   Oh, could the transport last!
>   I think of thee, and what thou art,
>   Thy Majesty, thy State;
>   And I keep singing in my heart—
>   Immaculate! Immaculate!"[1]

---

1   Faber, Hymn for the Feast of the Immaculate Conception.

And you have been taught to say then, more frequently than on other days, the little prayer which Our Lady loves:

> O Mary, conceived without sin, pray for us who have recourse to thee.

On the feast of the Nativity of Our Lady, we keep the Queen's Birthday, and so on.

All the feasts which bear the names of events in the life of the Blessed Mother and her Divine Son are, as I said, easily understood; but some others may need an explanation, and so I will try to tell you, as briefly as possible, the meaning of some of them.

On the 24th of May comes the feast of Our Lady Help of Christians. This was instituted by the Holy Pope Pius VII, in thanksgiving for his deliverance from imprisonment and many serious dangers.

On the 16th of July we keep the feast of Our Lady of Mount Carmel, to commemorate the apparition of the Blessed Mother to a Carmelite monk named St. Simon Stock, to whom Mary showed the scapular, and told him to get people to wear it in her honor. If you have not yet been enrolled, get a pair of brown scapulars and ask a priest to enroll you as soon as possible.

For August 5, you will find the feast of Our Lady ad Nives marked in the Church's Calendar. Now you will think "Our Lady ad Nives" a very odd name for a feast until you are told that "*ad Nives*" means "of the Snows," and that many hundreds of years ago Our Lady wished a church to be built in her honor on a certain hill in Rome. To mark the very spot on which it was to be erected, she caused a shower of snow to fall just there—and nowhere else. A fall of snow on the 5th of August is, and was, a very unusual thing in Rome. The temptation is great to tell you the whole story and many others, but space is wanting. In another book,[1] you can learn more about the feasts of Our Lady of Mercy, Our Lady of Perpetual Succor, Our Lady of Good Counsel, and Our Lady of Lourdes.

And now that you have learned something more about the feasts of Our Lady, try to keep them well, and on those days above all others do nothing that can dishonor the Queen.

If you are so happy as to have made your First Communion, and show great love for your Mother in heaven, perhaps you may obtain permission to receive her Divine Son on her feasts. If that wonderful happiness is still in store for you, then on the feasts of Our Lady make what is called a *Spiritual Communion;* and sometimes, Children, say a *Hail Mary* to the Queen for me.

---

1 *The Queen's Festivals* by Mother Mary St. Peter.

Chapter II

The Queen's Titles

E often hear people speak of the "Titles of Mary," but if asked to explain what is meant by those words, it would not be quite easy to do so.

There was once a king of France who was supposed to be a very clever man, so that he made his kingdom a great deal larger than he found it—chiefly by seizing on other people's lands. Yet he was extremely foolish in regard to this very matter of the Titles of the Queen. This king—he was called Louis XI—imagined that he was very devout to Our Lady. He wore a number of little leaden images of the Blessed Mother stuck inside the band of his hat; and when he wished very much to succeed in any enterprise he was about to undertake, he set his hat before him on the table, knelt down, and entreated Our Lady to help him. This was quite right—and wise too, of course—if the project he had at heart was good. If it was bad, as was the case more often than not, then the practice was not only evil, but also most insulting to the Queen.

Well, once Louis XI wished very much to get possession of the property of one of his neighbors, and he knelt before his hat turning a little image of Our Lady of Cléry toward the front. Then he promised Our Lady of Cléry that if she would only grant him success, he would give her a large sum of money. Then he suddenly became afraid that Our Lady of Embrun, another title by which he was accustomed to invoke the Mother of God, would become jealous, and giving his hat a twirl to bring Our Lady of Embrun to the front, he cried out: "O Lady of Embrun! Do not be angry because I vowed a gift to Our Lady of Cléry! The next time you help me you shall have just as much."

Now even a baby can see how foolish that was. As if Our Lady of Cléry were one person and Our Lady of Embrun somebody else. The fact is that they were the titles of two celebrated images of the Queen which were venerated in the churches of Cléry and Embrun. And this came of not understanding the Titles of the Queen.

But what *is* a title?

The word really means the right a person may have to own or possess something. If you repeat the whole catechism, for instance, without making more than three mistakes, you are *entitled*—or have a title to—a prize. The girl who passes through all the classes with honor has a right—or title to—a diploma on leaving school.

But the more general use of the word title is to signify a name bestowed on a person in addition to that which he already possesses, in token of some deed by which he has distinguished himself; or to mark a position of rank. Thus we give the title "Discoverer of America" to Christopher Columbus; that of "Father of his Country" to George Washington; and Queen Isabella of Castile is entitled "The Catholic" because she drove out the infidels and reestablished the true faith in Spain. Columbus had, besides, the title of Admiral which showed his rank in the Spanish Navy; Washington was President, and Isabella was Queen.

People may also derive titles from the places of their birth, as Henry VI was called Henry of Windsor because he was born in Windsor Castle; or from lands, houses, or other property belonging to them. Many of the old French nobles bore titles of this kind, which afterward became family names.

I am afraid you find much of this rather tiresome, but you do not wish to be as silly as Louis XI, do you? And you do wish to learn as much as you can about the Queen. The study of her titles will help you to know her much better, and I think the worst is over now. What I want you to understand is that Our Lady's titles are given her for just such reasons as those I have set down.

You know, or, at least you sometimes say, the Litany of the Blessed Virgin, which we call the *Litany of Loreto*. Now this Litany is really a long list of *titles*, and each one of them, if you think about it for even a little while, will teach you a great deal about the Blessed Mother—what she is, what she does, what she can do, and what she has suffered for love of us—because her Son loved us.

Loreto is the name of the Church which covers the house that once stood at Nazareth and sheltered the Holy Family for so many years. It is believed to have been carried by Angels from Palestine at the time of the Crusades, and after having been removed from one place to another several times, it at last rested on the spot where it may be seen to-day. The Holy House is, itself, very small, and a large Church was built over it.

Once the office of sacristan in this Church was given to a holy old man who loved the Queen better than anything and anyone, excepting her Divine Son. Now, when he was lighting the candles on her Altar, and there were a great many of them, he pleased himself by calling Our Lady all the sweet names he could think of that suited her—and what sweet name does not? There are always worshipers at Loreto, and after a while the people got into the habit of repeating the names after the old sacristan. Then you might have heard a murmur all through the Church while the candles were being lighted: "Holy Mary, Pray for us;" "Holy Mother of God, Pray for us;" and so on. By degrees the *Kyrie eleison* and the invocations to the Three Persons of the adorable Trinity were added, and so the prayers of the good old sacristan grew into the Litany of Loreto. In time, it became known and used throughout the Church.

Not all the titles were put in by the old sacristan, however. Pope Pius V inserted the invocation "Help of Christians" after a great battle in which the infidels were overcome, thanks to the intercession of Mary. Pope Pius IX added "Queen conceived without stain of original sin," and Pope Leo XIII added "Queen of the Most Holy Rosary."

You often hear the Blessed Mother spoken of as Our Lady of Lourdes. That title is taken from the name of a place. The Queen actually appeared in 1858 to a young country girl named Bernadette, in the village of Lourdes, situated in the South of France. A fountain of water sprang up in the place, which has the miraculous property of healing the diseases of those who bathe in the fountain, or even drink of the water if they cannot get to Lourdes.

A little boy in England had his eye accidentally injured by a playmate, and the London doctors—they were very clever men—agreed that it must be taken out, as the sight was gone and unless the injured eye were removed, the other would be lost also. But a Novena was made, some water from Lourdes was given to the little boy, and nine days later, when the oculists examined the eye, behold! it was cured. There was only a tiny white spot left to show where the point of a toy arrow had entered.

The Queen is sometimes invoked as "Our Lady of Good Counsel," and there is a beautiful picture called by that title. We ask Our Lady of Good Counsel to help us particularly when we are puzzled to know what is best for us to do, or how to do something—a difficult problem, for example. There is a pretty story to tell about that picture, but we must not take time for it now.

"Our Lady of Perpetual Succor" is the title of another picture that is not so very pretty. I suppose the first picture of the kind was painted by someone whom Our Lady loved very much, for she loves the picture and is ready to grant any favor that would be good for us, if we ask her to do so when kneeling before it. You know the picture. It is that in which the Holy Child seems to be losing His shoe.

There is a great temptation to tell you more about the titles of the Queen—and pretty stories are attached to most of them. But they would take up a whole book in themselves, so that will have to wait. Try to learn as much as you can about all that belongs to her, for the more you know of her the more you will love her, and the better you will love and serve her Divine Son. So you will earn a right to a title—that of Devout Children of Mary—and to a place very near her glorious throne in your true Country, which is Heaven.

Chapter III

The Queen's Praises

ONG ago, before books were printed, and when even grown-up people learned all that they knew either from their own observation, or from what others told them in story or song, there lived in the courts of kings certain persons who were called minstrels or Bards.

It was the business of these persons to make poems in praise of their sovereign, setting forth his wisdom, courage, riches, and power; and telling all his noble deeds. These poems were written down and were sung at banquets and on other great occasions, so that all might hear the praises of the king. Even now a poet is appointed to write verses for the sovereign on his birthday, or when anything of importance happens. This poet is called the Laureate. You have all heard of Lord Tennyson, who was Poet Laureate in the reign of Queen Victoria.

It was not unusual in ancient times for kings themselves to like to hear the songs and stories made about them. Perhaps you remember how King Assuerus, in the book of Esther, when he could not sleep one night, ordered his servants to read the history of his own reign for his amusement.

Now, if in all ages it has been the custom for men to sing the praises of their sovereign, what should be done for the King of kings—and for His Mother, Mary the Queen?

Is it not right and fitting that their praises should be spoken and sung?

And so indeed they have been from the beginning, and will be to the end of time.

The Prophets and other inspired writers of the Old Testament were the first to sing the praises of Mary. Much that they wrote is so beautiful that the Church has taken whole passages from the Sacred Scriptures, and set them in the Offices and in the Mass wherewith she honors Mary on her festivals. You will know and love them well when you are a little older, I trust.

However, there are praises of the Queen which you and every Catholic child must use every day, and these ones you can and ought to understand, at least to a certain extent.

Then, too, you should know the names of some of the Poets Laureates of Mary. The first name I will tell you is that of the Angel Gabriel, the Guardian Angel of the Queen.

When he brought to her the tidings that God had chosen her to become His Mother, Gabriel said: "Hail Mary, full of grace; the Lord is with thee." Then St. Elizabeth added later: "Blessed art thou among women; and blessed is the Fruit of thy womb—Jesus."

So was made the first part of the *Hail Mary*.

You say it every day and many times a day. Have you ever thought that in saying it you are reciting the praises of Mary the Queen?

When the old Bards sang or spoke the praises of their master, they very often added a petition for something they wanted themselves, as it was quite natural they should. What they did in their own interest, we do by command of our Master and Lord, who said: "Ask, and you shall receive;"[1] and, "Whatsoever you shall ask in prayer, believing, you shall receive."[2] So as the first part of the Hail Mary is a praise of the Queen, the second part is a prayer for ourselves. Did you ever think of this?

There was a dear old Irish woman who "made the round of her beads" twice every day, she said. "The first time I say the whole of it, and that's for my own soul and the souls of all poor sinners," she explained; "but the second time I say only the first half of the Hail Mary, and I give her that for herself, since it isn't manners to be asking for something all the time."

Our Queen is right royal, and loves to be giving with both hands, all the time, but let us never forget

1 John 16:24.   2 Matthew 21:22.

that she is in all things like her Son, and He felt hurt when, of ten lepers he had healed, only one returned to give thanks; and "this was a Samaritan."[1]

To say or sing the praises of Mary is our fashion of thanking her, so be sure always to say the first part of the *Hail Mary* as attentively as you can.

So many of your prayers to Our Lady are made up of *Hail Marys* that if you know how to say that with attention, you know how to say them all.

The *Angelus* you say three times to assure the Queen that you have not forgotten her, even in the midst of study or play. How do you say it? Father Faber declares that only too many people gabble it as if they were "praying against a bell."[2] Sometimes you say the Rosary—which was arranged by St. Dominic—with its grand "Glory be to the Father," and sweet "Hail, Holy Queen." Before it is ended, are you playing with your beads or your fingers, weary of praising the Queen?

The hymns to Our Lady that you sing are praises of Mary. Do you ever begrudge the time and trouble it costs you to learn them? And when known, do you sing them now and then so carelessly that in the words there is no sense whatever, and the angels who make such grand music in heaven must shudder at the sounds which you call tune?

And now I must say no more of the honors of the Queen. There are many more that you know and can think about, as the Crowning of her statue in her own

1   Luke 17:16.   2   *Spiritual Conferences*, 1859.

month of Mary; the May Devotions and Processions; the prayers you say daily at home and at school. And of this you may rest assured: that none of us can pay her any honor she will value so highly as that of showing in our lives that we are the true Children and devoted servants of our glorious Mother and Mistress—MARY THE QUEEN.

Feasts Of Our Lady

Espousals of the Blessed Virgin Mary.

January 23

Purification of the Blessed Virgin Mary.

February 2

Feast of Our Lady of Lourdes.

February 11

The Annunciation of the Blessed Virgin Mary.

March 25

Feast of Our Lady of Good Counsel.

April 26.

Feast of Our Lady of Perpetual Succor.

April 27.

Feast of Our Lady of Fatima.

May 13

Feast of Our Lady Help of Christians.

May 24

The Visitation of the Blessed Virgin Mary.

July 2.

Feast of Our Lady of of Mount Carmel.

July 16.

Feast of Our Lady ad Nives.

August 5.

The Assumption of the Blessed Virgin Mary.

August 15.

The Nativity of the Blessed Virgin Mary.

September 8.

The Holy Name of Mary.

Sunday after Nativity.

Feast of Seven Dolors of the Blessed Virgin Mary.

Third Sunday of September.

Our Lady of Mercy.

September 24.

Feast of the Holy Rosary.

First Sunday in October.

Maternity of the Blessed Virgin Mary.

Second Sunday in October.

Purity of the Blessed Virgin Mary.

Third Sunday in October.

Patronage of the Blessed Virgin Mary.

Fourth Sunday in October.

The Immaculate Conception.

December 8.

The Expectation of the Nativity.

December 18.

Additional titles available from

St. Augustine Academy Press

Books for the Traditional Catholic

Titles by Mother Mary Loyola:

Blessed are they that Mourn
Confession and Communion
Coram Sanctissimo (Before the Most Holy)
First Communion
First Confession
Forgive us our Trespasses
Hail! Full of Grace
Heavenwards
Home for Good
Jesus of Nazareth: The Story of His Life Written for Children
Questions on First Communion
The Child of God: What comes of our Baptism
The Children's Charter
The King of the Golden City
The Little Children's Prayer Book
The Soldier of Christ: Talks before Confirmation
Trust
Welcome! Holy Communion Before and After
With the Church

Titles by Father Lasance:

The Catholic Girl's Guide
The Young Man's Guide

Tales of the Saints:

A Child's Book of Saints by William Canton
A Child's Book of Warriors by William Canton
Legends & Stories of Italy by Amy Steedman
Mary, Help of Christians by Rev. Bonaventure Hammer
Page, Esquire and Knight by Marion Florence Lansing
The Book of Saints and Heroes by Leonora Lang
Saint Patrick: Apostle of Ireland
The Story of St. Elizabeth of Hungary by William Canton

Check our Website for more:
www.staugustineacademypress.com

THE SEAT OF WISDOM SERIES

Learn the lesser-known traditional teachings of our Faith
An excellent supplement to any catechesis program!

BY MOTHER MARY ST. PETER

of the Society of the Holy Child Jesus
originally published between 1905 and 1910

Mary the Queen:
A Life of the Blessed Mother for her Little Ones

The Lessons of the King:
Parables Made Plain for His Little Ones

Talks with the Little Ones about the Apostle's Creed

The Queen's Festivals:
An Explanation of the Feasts of the Blessed Virgin Mary

The Story of the Friends of Jesus

The Story of the Miracles of Our Lord

The Gift of the King:
A Simple Explanation of the Doctrines & Ceremonies
of the Holy Sacrifice of the Mass

The Laws of the King:
Talks on the Commandments

"The Sisters of the Holy Child in America have made a distinctly valuable
contribution to religious literature for children. There are nearly a dozen
neatly printed and illustrated volumes...which are, like Mother Loyola's
books, a real joy and help to the child."

—The Ecclesiastical Review, July 1910.

"[Mother Mary St. Peter] has a very clear, pleasing style; and she knows
youthful hearts thoroughly. Her talks about the Commandments are
excellent, not saying too much, and showing a great deal of shrewdness and
discretion in her way of putting things. We are sure that the whole series,
of which this is the newest volume, must be very useful for those who are
responsible for the instruction of the young."

—The Irish Monthly, July 1910.